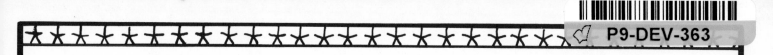

The International Design Library ™

EGYPTIAN DESIGNS

by Catherine Calhoun

Stemmer
House
PUBLISHERS, INC.
Owings Mills, Maryland

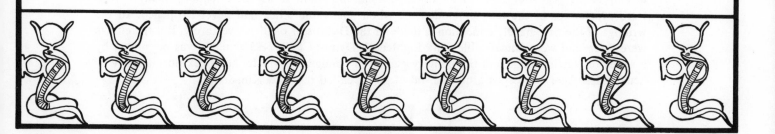

Introduction

THE MAGIC AND BEAUTY of Egyptian art crosses the boundaries of race, culture and language. One needs no explanation in order to enjoy it. However, since the examples in this book span the history of Egyptian civilization from the First Dynasty to the Twenty-Second, the development of that civilization is enormously interesting.

History

Throughout its history, Egypt thought of and referred to itself as "The Two Lands." The area that bordered the Mediterranean and contained the Delta of the Nile was known as Lower Egypt. Comprising roughly one quarter of the total land, this quarter was the richest, most fertile area. Its population was mixed, owing to the influx of Lybians from the west and Asiatics from the east—cosmopolitan in flavor.

In predynastic times the socio-political organization of Egypt was in the form of small city-states. These were held together in a rather loose confederation in Lower Egypt. By contrast, the more rural Upper Egypt, which extended from somewhere just south of Cairo all the way to the first cataract of the Nile, was a much more unified country. It was also much more isolated and much harsher a country than its northern neighbor. Most of its land area was uninhabitable desert. The exception was the trough of the Nile.

Around 3100 B.C. the two lands were united. In legend the feat was accomplished by King Menes. In reality it was most probably one of the first Pharaohs of the first dynasty who affected this union. Little comes to us from this distant time. Speculation has it that this was a period of transition concerned primarily with consolidation of power and creation of a workable form of government. By the time of the Third Dynasty the process was complete, and Egypt settled into an era of increasing prosperity and security. It was a time when Egypt was certain of her uniqueness and superiority. She was the center of the universe and home of the gods where one of their number, the Pharaoh, walked the earth, and ruled her with divine wisdom. This was Egypt's Golden Age, and it lasted until the Sixth Dynasty, a period of about 700 years.

The advent of the Seventh Dynasty, c. 2181 B.C., saw a much-changed Egypt. The power of the Pharaoh began to disintegrate, and the once strong, unified government collapsed. The two lands split apart and shattered into a number of individual principalities. Pharaohs came and went in rapid succession. It is probable that Egypt's troubles were aggravated by vast climactic changes that were sweeping across Africa and Asia at this time. Famine was rife. Marauding bands of starving peoples crossed Egypt's borders in search of food, and she had little defense against them. On the home front, the Nile was being particularly uncooperative: flooding too much one year and not nearly enough the next. The Pharaoh, as a god, was supposed to be in control of the Nile and obviously was not—a fact that further weakened the Egyptian people's belief in their ruler.

Eventually the lean times passed, and by the Eleventh Dynasty, c. 2133 B.C., Egypt had been reunited under the rule of a southern pharaoh who had established his capitol at Thebes in Upper Egypt. Peace and stability were restored and continued for roughly 300 years. Then the country was weakened once again, this time by rival pharaohs in Lower Egypt. Asiatic peoples, commonly known as Hyksos, infiltrated the Delta and gradually gained more and more power until one of their number was able to seize control of the entire land. There followed an unhappy period of humiliation for Egypt. The impossible, the unimaginable, had happened. Egypt, the center of the universe, the chosen home of the gods, had been subjugated by an inferior foreigner!

These usurping kings held their power over Egypt until the late Seventeenth Dynasty. Then, at long last, Egypt shook off her lethargy, rose up, and smote down the offending enemy. Afterwards, historians of the time pretended the whole miserable affair had never happened. In the writings of the time hardly a mention is made of the Hyksos or of their overthrow. But the effects were there and were unavoidable. The Eighteenth Dynasty (1567-1320 B.C.) was populated by a series of warrior kings and the military gained in strength. Egypt looked back nostalgically to her Golden Age, but forged a new period of glory, called the New Kingdom.

Increased contact with the outside world brought Egypt a degree of wealth and prosperity unparalleled in her long history. Frequent military campaigns kept her constantly supplied with a slave work force and, in peacetime, her large standing army added to this labor pool. Now, more than ever, Egypt had the financial and physical means with which to indulge her taste for the opulent, luxurious and colossal. This stand in glory lasted until the Twenty-First Dynasty, when Egypt once more experienced a period of civil strife. There followed a series of dynasties composed of a variety of foreign-born kings. These kings molded their beliefs and tastes to those of Egypt, and many times during the next ten or twelve dynasties the country rose to new and glorious heights under their leadership.

The people of ancient Egypt were most fundamentally influenced by the land in which they lived. It was a well-ordered land. The life-giving Nile was the center of their world. The predictable cycle of inundating and receding waters gave them fertile soil in which to plant their crops and marked the change of seasons in their year. Its south-to-north flow divided the country in half lengthways. Overhead the airborne bark of the sun sailed across the sky at right angles to the path of the Nile. The vast, uninhabitable deserts which stretched away to either side of the Nile valley cut Egypt off from her neighbors and protected and isolated her. In this haven the Egyptians grew to feel secure and confident of their unique place at the center of the world. They did not doubt that Egypt would go on for eternity, unchanged and untouched.

Their religion grew out of and was inexorably intertwined with this land and with the life they led. It was a vibrant, colorful religion, steeped in magic and populated by a rich variety of deities. The myths which surrounded these deities reinforced the Egyptians' perception of their world. In the story of creation, one of the events described is the fashioning by one of the gods of a regime of order, out of what had hitherto been nothing but chaos. The god then gave this regime into the care of man and the god-pharaoh to protect and maintain. In an effort to preserve this revered order, the Egyptians strove for moderation, patience and benevolence in every aspect of their lives.

These, briefly, were the factors which shaped the mind and spirit of the ancient Egyptian. But how did these factors translate themselves into art? Let us begin with their visual perception of the world. With the paths of the Nile and the sun crossing at right angles, neatly dividing the land, and the emphasis on order in their religion, the Egyptians developed a rectilinear view of the earth. The land formed a base above which stretched the sky, held aloft by a pole at each of four corners. This image of the world is repeated over and over again, symbolically, in Egyptian paintings and reliefs. Often a decorated wall of a tomb—or less frequently, a temple—was enclosed within four lines which represented the earth, sky and supporting poles. In plates 4 through 7 you will find clear examples of this artistic device. Their strong sense of order also influenced the placement of elements within a panel and gave to their art that decorative, pattern-oriented design character that we have come to associate with it. Every panel was divided horizontally to give each scene in a sequence of events a base line on which to rest. The hieroglyphic description of events would be laid out in neat rows, often with vertical lines separating each column of writing. See plates 6, 14, 15 and 24 for examples of these two aspects.

The impression of pattern in Egyptian art was strengthened by the way in which each individual character was represented, as well as by its placement in the overall picture. In a group scene the individuals would be depicted not in the random poses one might view in reality but in repetitive, stylized poses. There was very little effort made to distinguish single individuals. For example, in scenes depicting conquered foreigners, an entire group of people would be represented by one character with the outstanding physical attributes and garb that the Egyptians associated with that particular nationality. Examples which illustrate this are in plates 11 and 22. The top two panels in plate 22 show the use of single figures to represent entire peoples. In the bottom panel, note that the figures of the three sons are virtually indistinguishable one from another. Both pages are good examples of the use of repetitive, stylized poses. Even when the individuals are of different nationalities or are carrying different burdens there is enough similarity to give that illusion of pattern.

The lack of individuality in characters and the stylized poses were not dictated by the Egyptians' sense of order alone. Their belief in Egypt as an eternal, unchanging entity demanded that they represent themselves and the occurrences of their life in a way which was equally eternal and unchanging. It was also believed that a picture contained the very essence of that which was depicted, and that the picture could be brought to life by means of magic. Therefore a scene or person would be shown as a composite of its most important aspects. The cover illustration, which also appears in plate 30, shows the garden pool as seen from an aerial view, and the surrounding trees as seen from a side view. People were shown with their heads, arms, hips and legs in profile, and their eyes and torsos in a frontal view. Very rarely was a person depicted as old, malnourished or worried. The ideal, which evolved during Egypt's Golden Age, was an individual captured for eternity at the prime of his life and the height of his prosperity, with a calm demeanor and an expression about his eyes which seemed to indicate a quiet contemplation of that eternity.

The ancient Egyptians were able to maintain their artistic principals almost without change for thousands of years because while there were individual artists striving for personal expression of transitory emotions, there were also craftsmen, working in studios, producing a traditional, very refined product. At first, this product existed almost exclusively within the domain of religion. In the early dynasties the overseer of the studios was a High Priest of Ptah, the god who was known as the "Creator," and it was the priest who was originally responsible for the design and execution of all works of art. Within the studios the artisans practiced their craft and handed down their knowledge and skills from one generation to another.

All of this may give the distinct impression that Egyptian art remained unchanged by the events which shaped the country's history. It is true that the Egyptians yearned to cling to the ideals of their past, and indeed did return to them over and over again throughout their history, but they were not unmoved by the forces of their own times.

During the Archaic Period and the Old Kingdom, a time of peace and security for Egypt, the Egyptians developed and perfected their artistic skill. Stylistically, they developed a number of devices which were to enjoy frequently renewed popularity throughout their history. These included the pose of the conquering king smiting an enemy kneeling before him (plate 2); the use of a frieze of cobras as both a decorative and a protective device (title page and plate 3); men with their left foot forward and women with both feet together (plate 18); portrayal of the deceased sitting before an offering table (plate 23); personification of the deceased's estates as men or women bearing provisions (plate 11). The tradition of portraying the Pharaoh with a calm, benign expression and in a quiet pose and, in contrast, showing his servants in attitudes of vigorous activity, began during these early dynasties.

Egypt's decline into the first Intermediate period, Seventh to Tenth Dynasties, saw an equal decline in art. In flavor it became more rustic, and in execution it became cruder and more obvious. Its saving grace lay in the fact that it was more lively and original than that of preceding dynasties. The design innovation of the era could be seen in the portrayal of the human form, now shown in an aggressive stance, with massive or—towards the end of the era—elongated limbs. The advent of the Eleventh Dynasty, the beginning of the Middle Kingdom, saw a resurgence of the arts. Quality, on the whole, continued to improve, though private works were often less admirable. Painting was more popular than reliefs. Scenes of warfare were common. Royal portraits were designed to be overbearing and awesome, and in place of the calm expression favored in earlier times the Middle Kingdom Pharaohs appear severe and aloof. The Second Intermediate period, with the invasion by the Hyksos, did little or nothing for the Egyptians' art. It was not until the Eighteenth Dynasty (1567-1320 B.C.), the New Kingdom, that Egyptian art rose again to glory.

The New Kingdom, with its wealth, prosperity and strong military protection, allowed the Egyptians to indulge themselves fully. The art of this period is more decorative, more elaborate, more colorful than ever before. This is the Egyptian art which is most commonly seen today and which appeals most strongly to people the world over. It represents a return to the values and traditions of the past, with the nostalgia regarding Egypt's Golden Age becoming even stronger. Unlike the dynasties which immediately preceded it, the Eighteenth Dynasty produced a high-quality art which was executed with precision and finesse. The style of their art was elegant and sophisticated and fluid of line. As the dynasty progressed, the art became livelier and there can be seen the beginnings of the realism which was so popular during the Amarna period.

The Amarna period began with the ascension of the Pharaoh Akhenaten (1379-c. 1362 B.C.). The art of the time took on a markedly realistic aspect. The Pharaoh and his family were depicted with all of their physical shortcomings (occasionally exaggerated) and in poses which were very human and transient. These poses, however secular and domestic they may appear, were in truth manifestations of Akhenaten's strong religious convictions. It was because of his belief in his own and his family's divinity that he could be portrayed in such a familiar manner. There was also some attempt made at showing perspective, which had hitherto been entirely lacking in Egyptian art, as well as differentiating right and left hands and feet. Most of these innovations were short-lived. With the demise of Akhenaten the Egyptians began to revert to a style which was familiar and comfortable. The art of the Ramesside era, Dynasties Nineteen and twenty, got off to a strong start. Quality reliefs were produced under the rule of Sethos I, and ambitious building projects were undertaken during the rule of Rameses II. After Rameses II, the quality of Egyptian art faltered and remained erratic to the end of the Twentieth Dynasty. The Twenty-first Dynasty saw the first of a long succession of foreign-born kings. These king's carried forward the traditions of Egyptian art, often raising it to new heights.

C. C.

List of Illustrations

12	Carved steatite and alabaster disk, probably used in a table game. The positioning of the animals on the disk serves to square off the space so that it conforms to the Egyptian view of the world as being contained within a rectangular area. Dynasty 1

13   Composite design. Top: A portion of a tiled wall whose design imitated that of the reed matting which decorated the walls of the deceased's house during his lifetime. From a tomb in the pyramid complex of King Djoser. Dynasty 3

Middle: Repetitive design found on Tut-ankh-amen's sarcophagus. Dynasty 18

Bottom: Design found on the sarcophagus of Ra-ur which imitates the facade of a house. Dynasty 5

14, 15   Uniting Egypt. Two gods bind the hieroglyphic symbol for union with the lotus flower of Lower Egypt and the papyrus flower of Upper Egypt.
P.14: Dynasty 12, from a stela of Sesostris I
P.15: Dynasty 19, from the temple of Ramses II at Abu Simbel
CENTERFOLD

Top: Painting of Geese from the tomb of Itat. Dynasty 4

Bottom: Copy of a painting in the tomb of Menna. Dynasty 18

18   From The Book of the Dead of Hunefer. Above, the sun god being received by seven figures of Thoth as a baboon and, below, the djed-column, symbol of Osiris, flanked by Isis on the left and Nephthys on the right. Dynasty 19

19   Composite of two panels from The Book of the Dead of Ani. On the left, Seker (a Memphite god of the dead often associated with Osiris) as a mummified falcon. On the right, the herd of heaven. Dynasty 18

20   Statue of King Mycerinus with the goddess Hathor (wearing heifer's horns and the solar disk) and the goddess of Diospolis Parva on either side of him. Dynasty 4

21   Pendant representing the Osirian triad (Horus, Osiris, and Isis) which belonged to Osorkon II, one of the Libyan Kings of Egypt. Dynasty 22

22   Necklace worn by Tut-ankh-amen during his life time. It features a pendant of a bark carrying the crescent and disk of the moon over the waters of the firmament, which are represented by a row of lotus flowers. The lotus and fringe of beads at the top of the drawing comprise a counterpoise, designed to hang down in back when the necklace was worn. Dynasty 18

23   Top: Broad collar of faience beads. Dynasty 17

Bottom: Necklace of glass frogs, a symbol of fertility during life and of rebirth after death. New Kingdom

24   Top: Relief of foreign captives. From the temple of Ramses II at Abu Simbel. Dynasty 19

Middle: Foreign captives from Tut-ankh-amen's chariot. Dynasty 18

Bottom: Portion of a panel showing the deceased's three sons.

25   Portrait of the deceased Princess Neferti-abet sitting before an offering table covered with slices of bread. Dynasty 4

26   Top: An ebony cosmetic box which belonged to Sit Hathor Yunet, a daughter of Sesostris II. Dynasty 12

Bottom: A chair which belonged to Queen Hetep-Heres. Dynasty 4

27   Golden throne of Tut-ankh-amen picturing himself and his Queen, Nefreteti. Dynasty 18

28   Two faces of beauty: Left, the Princess Nofret and, right, the Queen Merit Amon. Dynasties 4 and 18, respectively

29   Roundel designs. Roundels were a common motif in Egyptian jewelry. Those in this design were taken from pieces made during the 4th through 18th dynasties.

30   Painting of a courtyard pool surrounded by date and dom palms, fig and pomegranate trees. Dynasty 18

31   Three figurines of animals. The two hippos date from the 17th Dynasty and were quite common at that time.
      The figure of the ibex and fawn is actually a vessel with the spout emerging from the adult animal's mouth. Dynasty 18

32   Gilded wood second coffin of Tut-ankh-amen. Dynasty 18

33   Repetitive designs. These are decorative designs that are found frequently throughout Egyptian art.

34   Triple alabaster lamp from Tut-ankh-amen's tomb. Dynasty 18

35   Alabaster vase from Tut-ankh-amen's tomb. Dynasty 18

36   Hieroglyphs. A page of incomplete spells from The Book of the Dead of Ani. Dynasty 18

37   Selected rows of designs from the coffin-board of a singer of Amun. The designs imitate the floral garlands that adorned the dead. Dynasty 21-22

38   Two scenes of music-making. Top: A wall painting in the tomb of Rekhmere at Thebes depicting a celebration for the dead. Dynasty 18
      Bottom: Painted relief in the tomb of Ny-kheft-ka at Saqqara. There is a theory that the two figures without instruments are indicating pitch to the two musicians by way of hand signals. Dynasty 5

39   Relief in the temple of Queen Hatshepsut at Der-el-bahari. Dynasty 18

I wish to thank especially the Curator of Egyptian and Classical Art at the Brooklyn Museum, and the staff of its Wilbur Library, who all gave generously of their time and knowledge in helping me to make this book as accurate as possible.

Plate 1

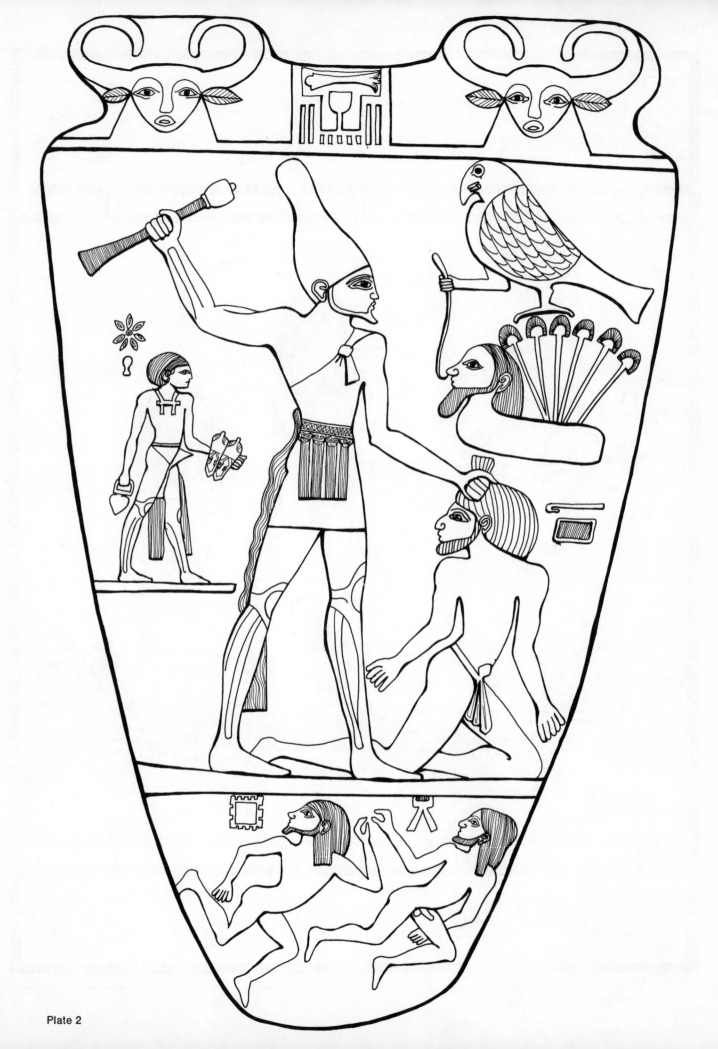

Plate 2

Plate 3

Plate 4

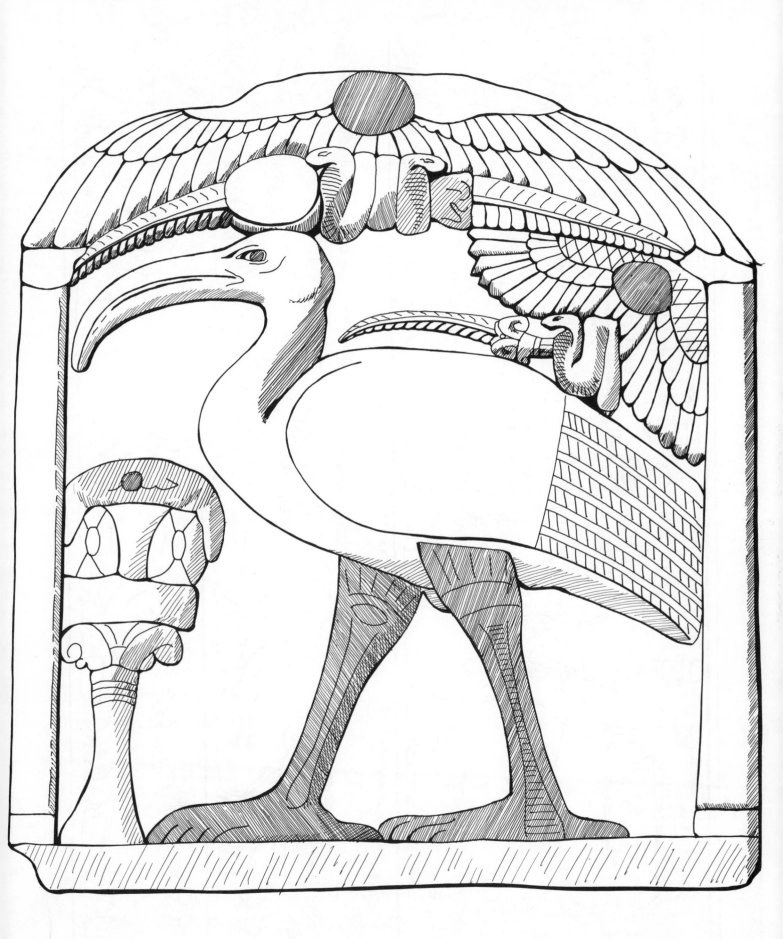

Plate 5

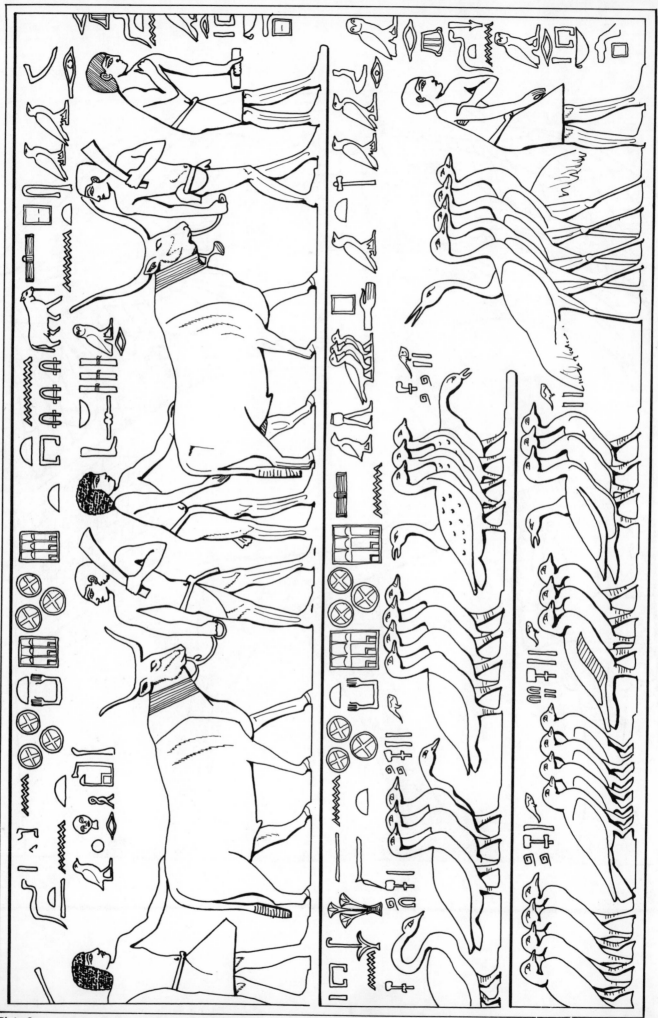

Plate 6

Plate 7

Plate 8

Plate 9

Plate 10

Plate 11

Plate 12

Plate 13

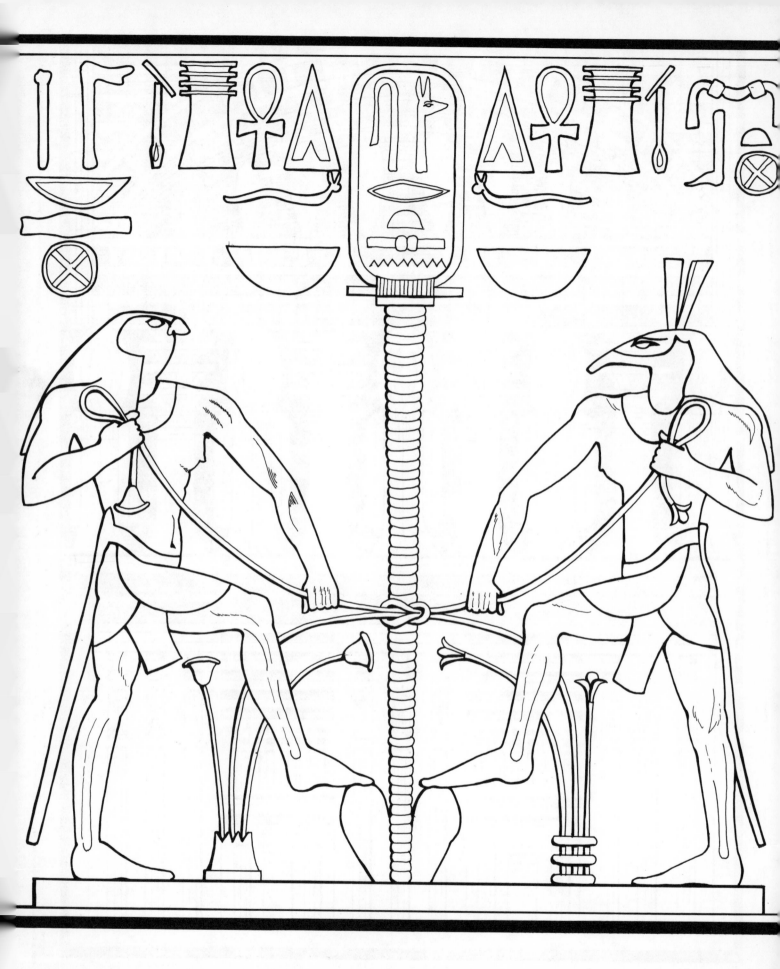

Plate 14

Plate 15

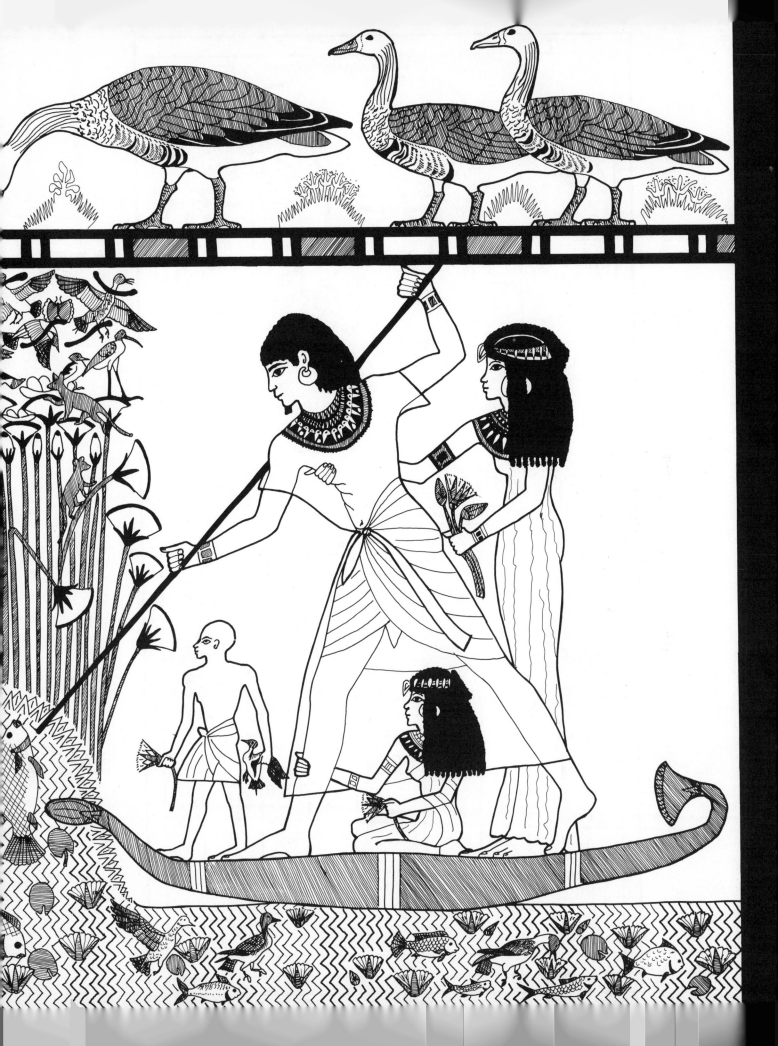

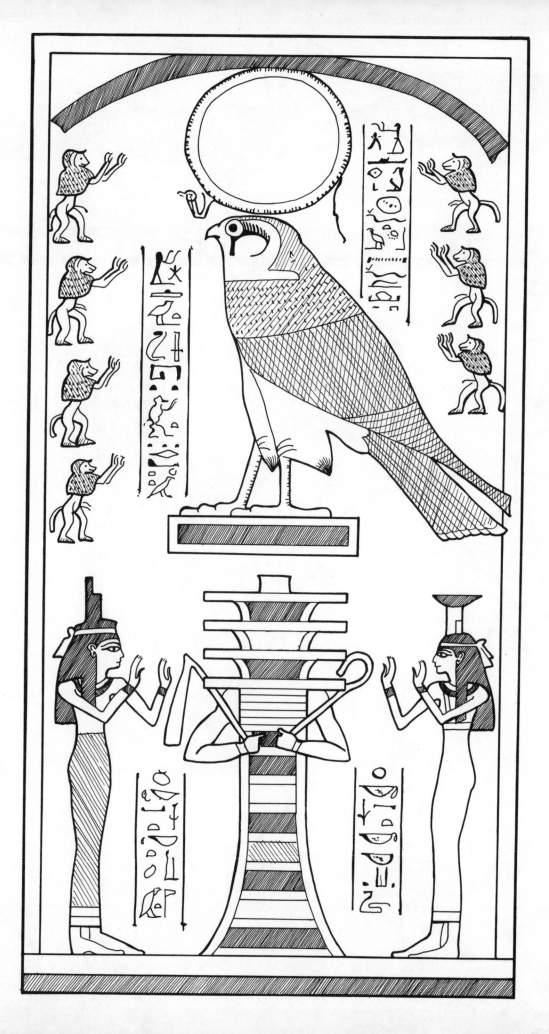

Plate 18

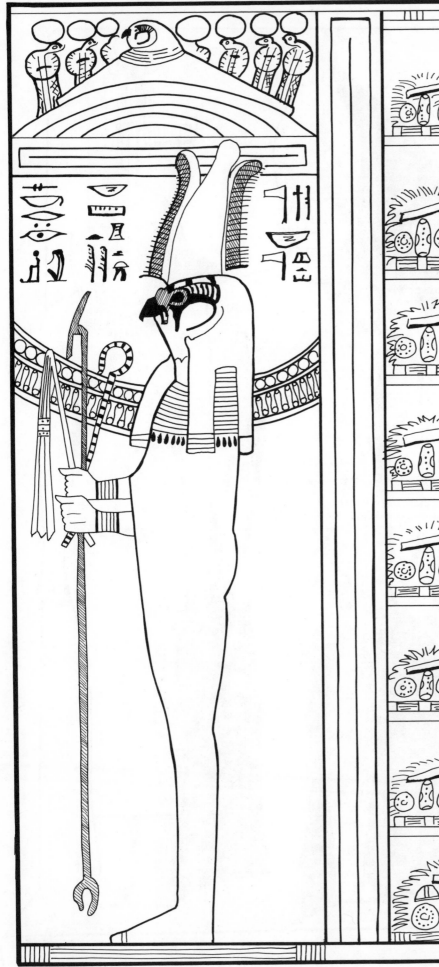
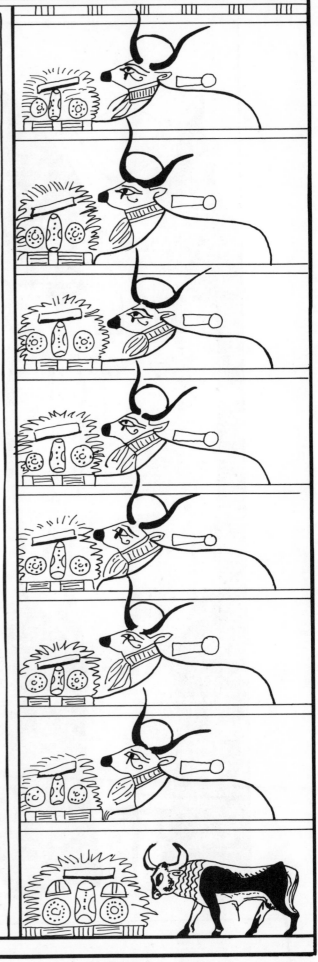

Plate 19

Plate 20

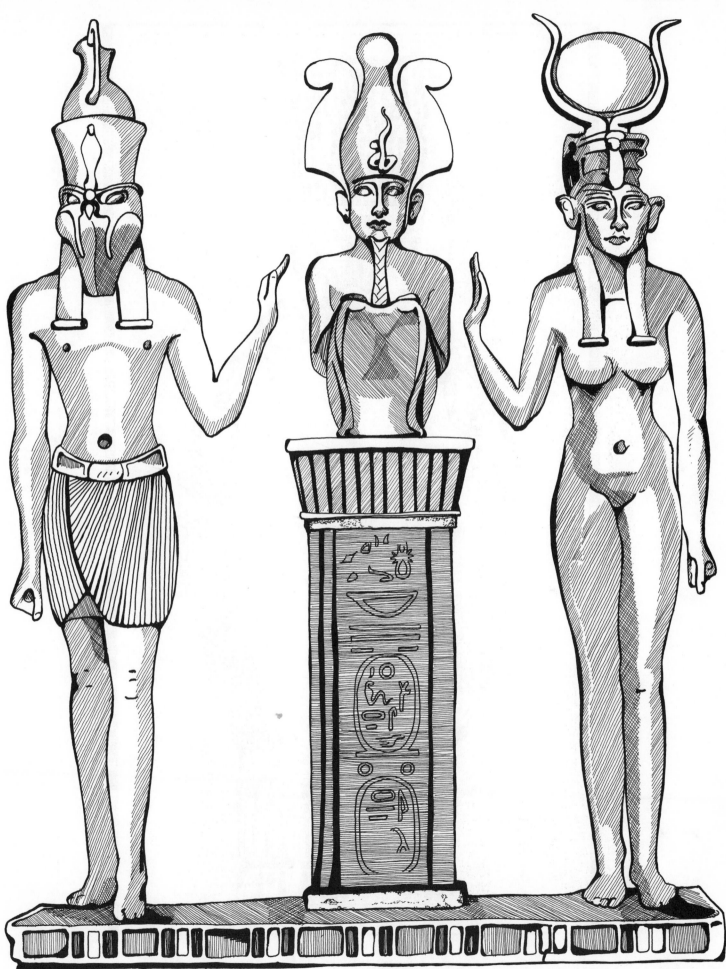

Plate 21

Plate 22

Plate 23

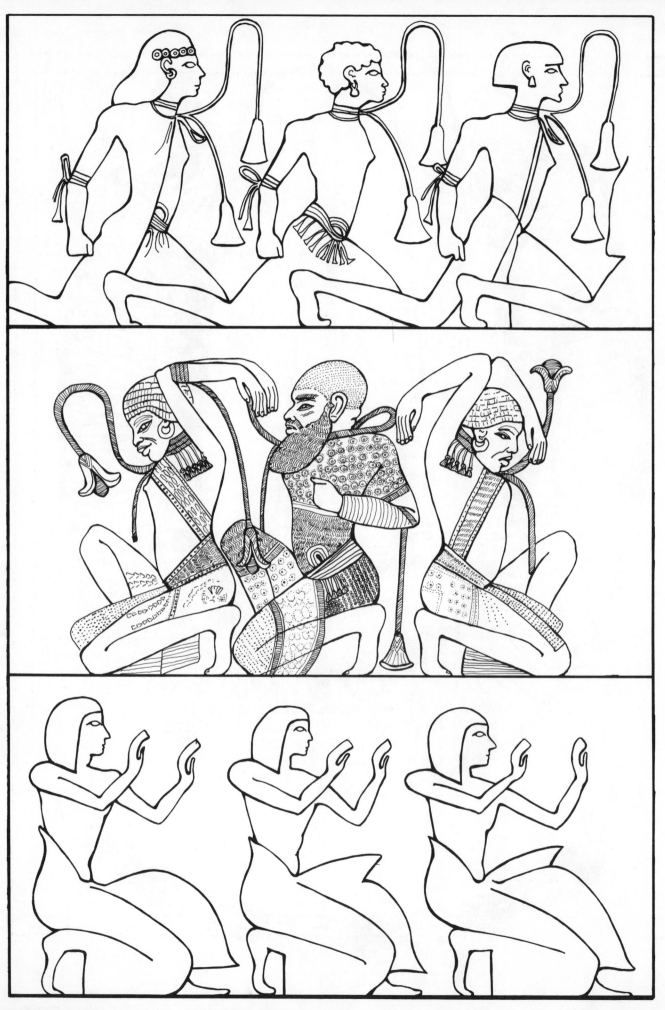

Plate 24

Plate 25

Plate 26

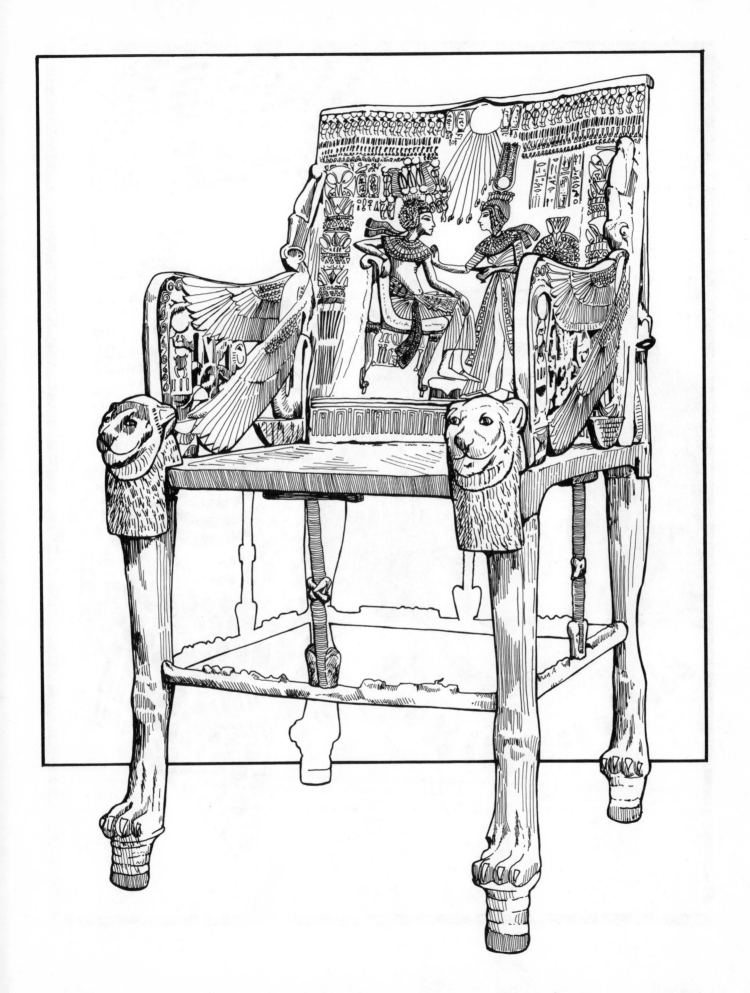

Plate 27

Plate 28

Plate 29

Plate 31

Plate 32

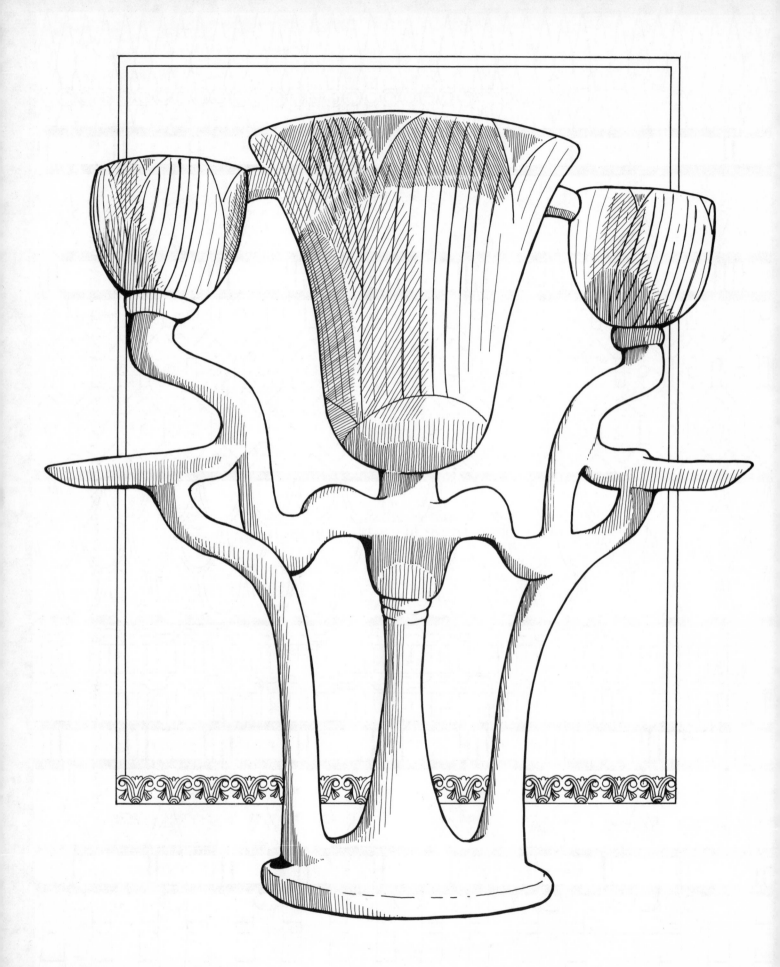

Plate 34

Plate 35

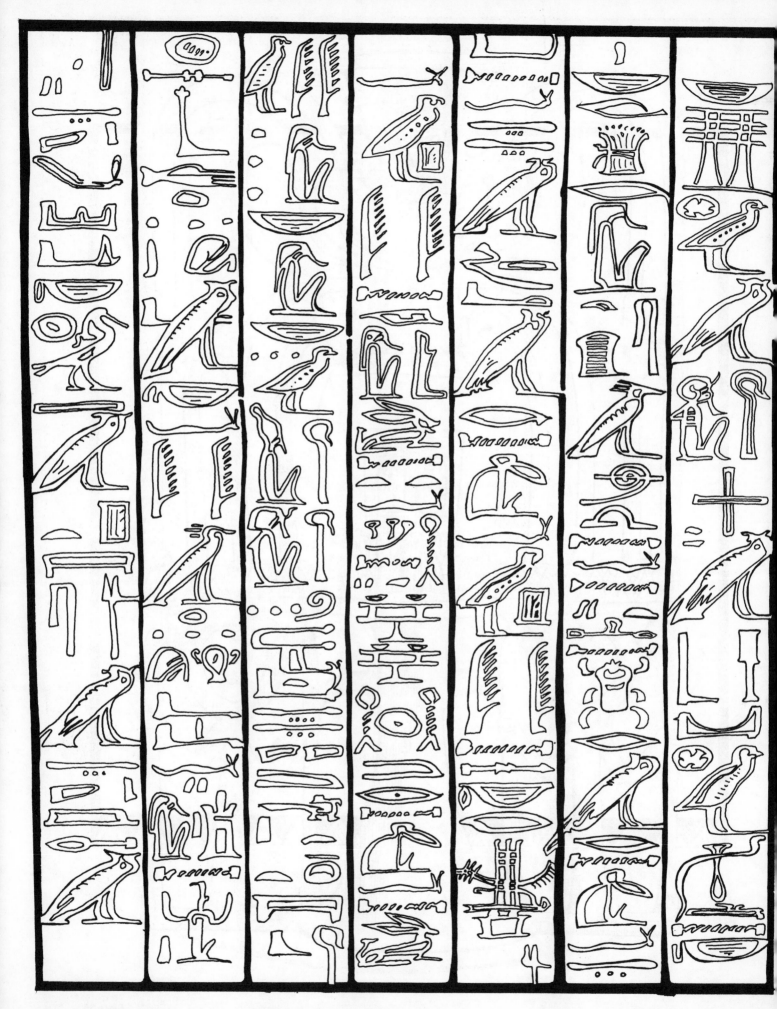

Plate 36

Plate 37

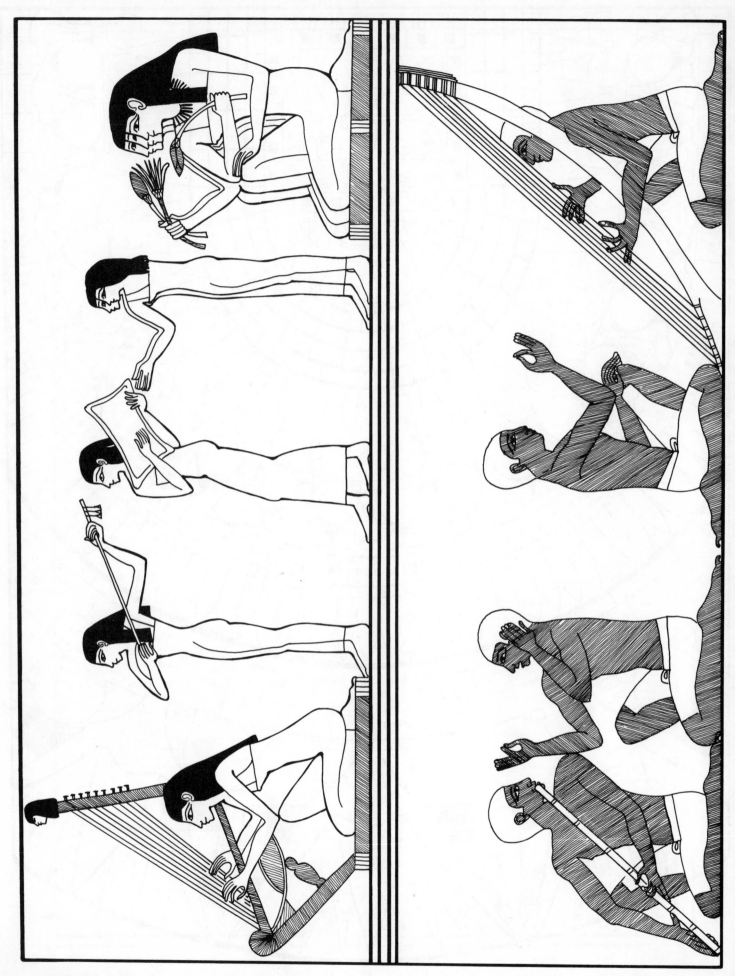

Plate 38

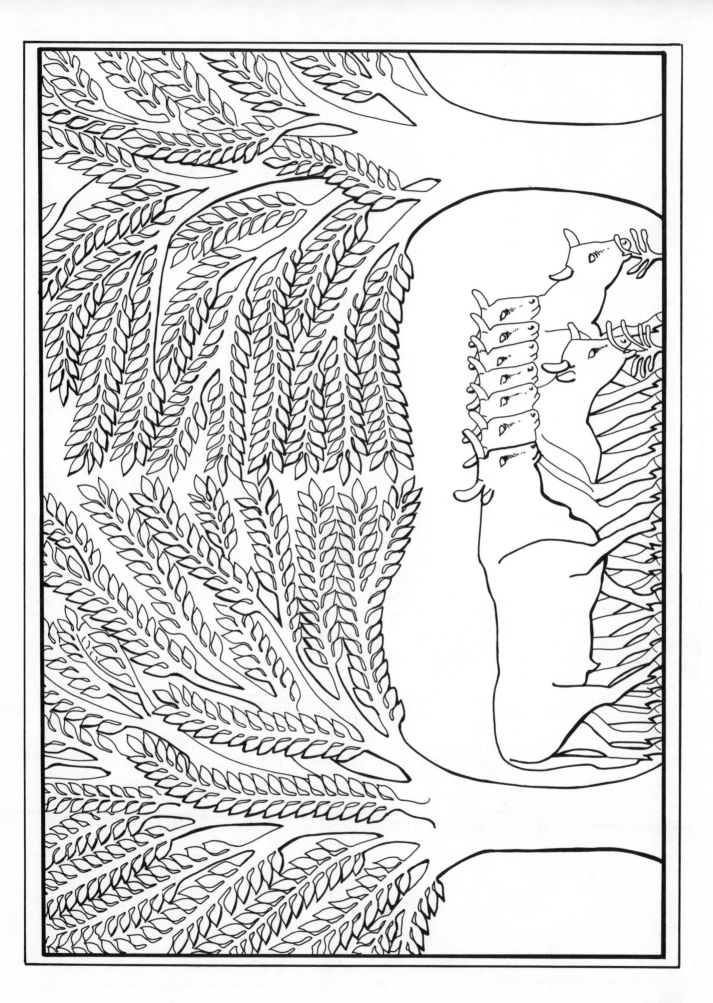

Plate 39

Designed by Barbara Holdridge
Composed by the Service Composition Company,
    Baltimore, Maryland
Covers printed by Rugby, Inc., Knoxville, Tennessee
Printed and bound by Port City Press, Inc.,
    Baltimore, Maryland, on 60-pound Williamsburg Offset